MW00423291

Acts: The Unbelievable Story of the Church

Christian Leaders Institute Publishing

Acts:The Unbelievable Story of the Church
Bible Study
By Steven Elzinga
Copyright ©2016 by the Christian Leaders Institute Publishing

CONTENTS

How this study works   4

Week/Lesson One
    The Church begins on Fire   9

Week/Lesson Two
    The Church needs Leaders   18

Week/Lesson Three
    Paul and Peter are Chosen   27

Week/Lesson Four
    The Church Expands   36

Week/Lesson Five
    The Church Explodes   45

Week/Lesson Six
    The Church on Trial   55

Week/Lesson Seven
    The Church on the World Stage   64

Supplemental Material One   72

Supplemental Material Two   73

Supplemental Material Three   74

How this study works ...

Basic Features:

- There is a total of 49 short lessons that follow 7 themes built from the book of Acts. Take note of the theme for the week at the top of each lesson.

- From your own Bible, read the scripture reference for the lesson of the day.

- Next you will find a box to write down anything that strikes you as you read the passage - i.e. an insight, a question, an interesting phrase - anything that catches your attention.

- In the next box, write down anything you can think of that God might be trying to say to you by the thing that got your attention (i.e. what you wrote in the first box).

- Next is a box for your prayers.

- People fasted in the book of Acts. You can too. Check the box if you did that today.

- Next you have an opportunity to write down a name of someone you might connect with and the manner of your connection.

- Finally, there are several questions that relate to the topic and scripture passage of the day that will help you think about and apply both to your life.

Unique Options:

Option One: Use this study like any other Bible study. There are 7 lessons for each of the 7 sections of the book of Acts for a total of 49 lessons. If your Bible study small group meets once a week, this study will last a year.

Unique Options:

Option Two: Use this study as a daily personal, marriage or family study. Since each lesson consists of 7 studies there is one for each day of the week. The whole Bible study would last 7 weeks.

Option Three: Use it as a daily personal, marriage or family study combined with a weekly group Bible study. As in option 2, you would do each of the seven lessons daily on your own (or with spouse and/or family). Then when your group meets you could ..

1. Pick one of the 7 lessons to do as a group lesson.

2. Let each group member pick a question or two from one of the 7 lessons that they did that week. They could read the question, tell why they picked it, and then that question would become a question for the whole group. If there were 10 people in the group you would have at least 10 questions for your group study.

3. Or the leader could pick questions from the 7 lessons of that week that he or she thinks would create the best discussion.

Option Four: Use any of the above options with the added component of a sermon that goes with each of the 7 sections in the book of Acts.

• Listen to the sermons at www.path2jesusway. org

• Use the sermons online as a research tool for your own sermon in your own church (See author's note on next page).

Note from the author of this Bible study:

As a Pastor, I slowly came to realize that many of the people attending my church were coming to the service with great expectations of what I might be able to do for them. They wanted to be fed spiritual food that would give them hope and strength for whatever they would face in the week ahead. So I did my best to feed them. But I soon discovered that no matter how well I did on Sunday to feed them, it was not enough to make it through the week.

God gave me a new thought: Why not teach them how to feed themselves? Instead of the people showing up to church having done no work at all for the spiritual food they were about to partake in, why not get them working on the sermon with me - all week long?

So I developed Bible Studies like this Acts Bible Study. The whole church studies the topic of the week and Bible passages that support that topic every day in their personal lives, their marriages and in their families. All of this is then reinforced and expanded on in small groups. And finally, the whole process culminates in the church service where the pastor gets to preach a powerful message that everyone has been involved with all week long.

In my church this approach has transformed my bench sitters into players, my attenders to activists, and my critical back-seat drivers to encouraging front-seat supporters.

Steve Elzinga
Pastor at Pathway Church &
Professor at CLI

Sirs, what must I do to be saved?
They replied,
Believe in the Lord Jesus, and you will be saved
—you and your household.

Acts 16:30,31

Date: _____

THE CHURCH BEGINS ON FIRE (Lesson #1)

❑ Read Acts 1:1-26

> *What struck you?*

> *What might God be saying to you?*

❑ Prayer

❑ I will fast today.

❑ I am going to connect w/ (visit, phone, email, facebook, note, card, have over) _____today.

❑ Questions:

1. How are you and your family being a witness in Jerusalem, Judea, and the rest of the world?

2. Just as the Church comes into existence, Jesus leaves for heaven. Why do you think Jesus leaves?

3. What do you think about casting lots for leadership positions?

THE CHURCH BEGINS ON FIRE (Lesson #1)

❏ Read Acts 2:1-41

What struck you?

What might God be saying to you?

❏ Prayer

❏ I will fast today.

❏ I am going to connect w/ (visit, phone, email, facebook, note, card, have over) _____today.

❏ Questions:

1. Why do you think the first manifestation of the Holy Spirit's coming was the disciples speaking in all the languages of the world?

2. What was so powerful about Peter's sermon?

3. By what number did the church grow that day?

Date: _____

THE CHURCH BEGINS ON FIRE (Lesson #1)

❑   Read Acts 2:42-47

> *What struck you?*

> *What might God be saying to you?*

❑ Prayer

❑ I will fast today.

❑ I am going to connect w/ (visit, phone, email, facebook, note, card, have over) _____ today.

❑ Questions:

1. What is significant about the people meeting both in the temple courts and in their homes?

2. Verse 46 starts with "Every day..." Why is this necessary for making close friendships?

3. What is the relationship between fellowship and church growth?

Date: _____

12

THE CHURCH BEGINS ON FIRE (Lesson #1)

❑ Read Acts 3:1-10

> *What struck you?*

> *What might God be saying to you?*

❑ Prayer

❑ I will fast today.

❑ I am going to connect w/ (visit, phone, email, facebook, note, card, have over) _____ today.

❑ Questions:

1. Why do we tend to think that what we need to make our lives happier is a little more money?

2. At this time in your life what do you think you really need to make your life happier?

3. Do you think the goal of your life should be happiness? If not happiness, what?

Date: _____

THE CHURCH BEGINS ON FIRE (Lesson #1)

❑ Read Acts 3:11-26

> *What struck you?*

> *What might God be saying to you?*

❑ Prayer

❑ I will fast today.

❑ I am going to connect w/ (visit, phone, email, facebook, note, card, have over) _____today.

❑ Questions:

1. Why are miracles always surprising?

2. Why do you think it was hard for the Jews to accept Jesus as the Messiah?

3. What sins in your life do you need to confess so that your life can be refreshed?

THE CHURCH BEGINS ON FIRE (Lesson #1)

❑ Read Acts 4:1-22

> *What struck you?*

> *What might God be saying to you?*

❑ Prayer

❑ I will fast today.

❑ I am going to connect w/ (visit, phone, email, facebook, note, card, have over) _____today.

❑ Questions:

1. Verse 4 says the number of believers grew to 5,000. Why do you think the church was growing so fast?

2. The religious leaders were astonished that Peter and John were courageous, unschooled, ordinary men who had been with Jesus. How might this be true of ordinary Christians today?

Date: _____

THE CHURCH BEGINS ON FIRE (Lesson #1)

❑ Read Acts 4:23-37

> *What struck you?*

> *What might God be saying to you?*

❑ Prayer

> *Pray for boldness in your witness*

❑ I will fast today.

❑ I am going to connect w/ (visit, phone, email, facebook, note, card, have over) _____ today.

❑ Questions:

1. Verse 29 speaks of threats to the Gospel. What threats keep us from spreading the Gospel to those around us?

2. Who needs a miracle from Jesus among those you know who do not go to church?

3. Can you pray for boldness for the next 5 weeks?

Date: _____

Sermon or Bible study notes on Lesson #1

Date: _____

Sermon or Bible study notes on Lesson #1

Date: _____

THE CHURCH NEEDS LEADERS (Lesson #2)

❑ Read Acts 5:1-42

> *What struck you?*

> *What might God be saying to you?*

❑ Prayer

> *Pray for boldness in your witness*

❑ I will fast today.

❑ I am going to connect w/ (visit, phone, email, facebook, note, card, have over) _____ today.

❑ Questions:

1. Why is the story of Ananias and Sapphira so troubling?

2. The threat of jail did not deter Peter and John from sharing the good news of Jesus. What deters you?

3. What is your reaction to verses 38 & 39?

Date: _____

THE CHURCH NEEDS LEADERS (Lesson #2)

❏ Read Acts 6:1-7

> *What struck you?*

> *What might God be saying to you?*

❏ Prayer

> *Pray for boldness in your witness.*
> *Pray for the leaders of your church.*

❏ I will fast today.

❏ I am going to connect w/ (visit, phone, email, facebook, note, card, have over) _____ today.

❏ Questions:

1. As the church grew so did the need for leaders. Why do you think they "chose" leaders instead of "electing" leaders?

2. Which do you think works better: Grow the church and then add new leaders, or, add new leaders and you will grow the church?

THE CHURCH NEEDS LEADERS (Lesson #2)

❑ Read Acts 6:8-15

> *What struck you?*

> *What might God be saying to you?*

❑ Prayer

> *Pray for boldness in your witness.*
>
> *Pray for the leaders of your church.*

❑ I will fast today.

❑ I am going to connect w/ (visit, phone, email, facebook, note, card, have over) _____ today.

❑ Questions:

1. Stephen was one of the seven chosen to supposedly do a diaconal role - help with food distribution. But here he is accused of doing great wonders and miraculous signs. What do you make of this?

2. Why do you think the religious leaders wanted to shut men like Stephen down?

Date: _____

THE CHURCH NEEDS LEADERS (Lesson #2)

❑ Read Acts 7:1-53

> *What struck you?*

> *What might God be saying to you?*

❑ Prayer

> *Pray for boldness in your witness.*
> *Pray for the leaders of your church.*

❑ I will fast today.

❑ I am going to connect w/ (visit, phone, email, facebook, note, card, have over) _____ today.

❑ Questions:

1. Why do you think Stephen starts his defense by talking about Abraham?

2. Why do you think Stephen spends most of his time talking about Moses?

3. At what point does Stephen's defense fall apart and why?

Date: _____

22

THE CHURCH NEEDS LEADERS (Lesson #2)

❏ Read Acts 7:54-60

> *What struck you?*

> *What might God be saying to you?*

❏ Prayer

> *Pray for boldness in your witness.*
> *Pray for the leaders of your church.*

❏ I will fast today.

❏ I am going to connect w/ (visit, phone, email, facebook, note, card, have over) _____ today.

❏ Questions:

1. At the moment of Stephen's greatest trial (he was about to be stoned) God gives him a sense of His presence. Have you ever had this kind of experience?

2. What does Stephen's last prayer tell you about Christianity?

3. Make a mental note of this man Paul.

Date: _____

THE CHURCH NEEDS LEADERS (Lesson #2)

❑ Read Acts 8:1-25

> *What struck you?*

> *What might God be saying to you?*

❑ Prayer

> *Pray for boldness in your witness.*
> *Pray for the leaders of your church.*

❑ I will fast today.

❑ I am going to connect w/ (visit, phone, email, facebook, note, card, have over) _____ today.

❑ Questions:

1. Philip was one of seven chosen to distribute food, but here he is preaching. Maybe all leaders are called to preach. What do you think about that?

2. Persecution led to the spread of the gospel. What is it going to take to get you to spread the gospel?

Date: _____

THE CHURCH NEEDS LEADERS (Lesson #2)

❏ Read Acts 8:26-40

> *What struck you?*

> *What might God be saying to you?*

❏ Prayer

❏ I will fast today.

❏ I am going to connect w/ (visit, phone, email, facebook, note, card, have over) _____ today.

❏ Questions:

1. Philip helped the Ethiopian understand what was in the Bible. Who in your world needs someone to explain the basics of the Word of God?

2. Do the lesson on pate 74 with your small group or on your own.

Date: _____

Sermon or Bible study notes on Lesson #2

Date: _____

Sermon or Bible study notes on Lesson #2

Date: _____

PAUL & PETER ARE CHOSEN (Lesson #3)

❑ Read Acts 9:1-42

> *What struck you?*

> *What might God be saying to you?*

❑ Prayer

> *Pray for boldness in your witness.*
> *Pray for the leaders of your church.*
> *Pray for your list.*

❑ I will fast today.

❑ I am going to connect w/ (visit, phone, email, facebook, note, card, have over) _____today.

❑ Questions:

1. Paul was converted rather dramatically. How were you converted?

2. Why is it so hard for people to believe that a person can change - or that you can change?

3. What is the purpose of miracles?

Date: _____

PAUL & PETER ARE CHOSEN (Lesson #3)

❑ Read Acts 10:1-23

> *What struck you?*

> *What might God be saying to you?*

❑ Prayer

> Pray for boldness in your witness.
> Pray for the leaders of your church.
> Pray for your list.

❑ I will fast today.

❑ I am going to connect w/ (visit, phone, email, facebook, note, card, have over) _____ today.

❑ Questions:

1. God orchestrated two visions to two different people in order to bring together two people that otherwise would have nothing to do with each other. When has this happened in your life? To whom on your "list" would you like to see this same thing happen?

Date: _____

PAUL & PETER ARE CHOSEN (Lesson #3)

❑ Read Acts 10:24-48

> *What struck you?*

> *What might God be saying to you?*

❑ Prayer

> *Pray for boldness in your witness.*
> *Pray for the leaders of your church.*
> *Pray for your list.*

❑ I will fast today.

❑ I am going to connect w/ (visit, phone, email, facebook, note, card, have over) _____today.

❑ Questions:

1. Why is it easy to start thinking that God loves one group of people over another?

2. Why were Peter's companions astonished that the Gentiles received the gift of the Holy Spirit?

3. What is our motivation in being "stingy" with God's love?

PAUL & PETER ARE CHOSEN (Lesson #3)

❏ Read Acts 11:1-18

> *What struck you?*

> *What might God be saying to you?*

❏ Prayer

> Pray for boldness in your witness.
> Pray for the leaders of your church.
> Pray for your list.

❏ I will fast today.

❏ I am going to connect w/ (visit, phone, email, facebook, note, card, have over) _____today.

❏ Questions:

1. Why do you think it was hard for the Jewish Christians to believe that God wanted to offer salvation to all people - Jews and Gentiles?

2. What evidence do you have in your life that God still speaks through angels and the Holy Spirit?

Date: _____

PAUL & PETER ARE CHOSEN (Lesson #3)

❑ Read Acts 11:19-29

> What struck you?

> What might God be saying to you?

❑ Prayer

> Pray for boldness in your witness.
>
> Pray for the leaders of your church.
>
> Pray for your list.

❑ I will fast today.

❑ I am going to connect w/ (visit, phone, email, facebook, note, card, have over) _____ today.

❑ Questions:

1. The name "Barnabas" means "son of encouragement." What place does encouragement have in the church? In your family? Your marriage? Your parenting? Your friendships?

2. The name "Christian" means "those who belong to Christ." How do you wear that name in public?

Date: _____

PAUL & PETER ARE CHOSEN (Lesson #3)

❑ Read Acts 12:1-19

> *What struck you?*

> *What might God be saying to you?*

❑ Prayer

> *Pray for boldness in your witness.*
> *Pray for the leaders of your church.*
> *Pray for your list.*
> *Who?*   *What?*

❑ I will fast today.

❑ I am going to connect w/ (visit, phone, email, facebook, note, card, have over) _____today.

❑ Questions:

1. The church prayed specifically for one person (Peter) and for a specific positive outcome for that person's situation (that Peter would be set free). Who can you specifically pray for? What specific positive outcome can you pray for?(see Who?.....What? in prayer box).

2. Why are we surprised when God answers prayer?

Date: _____

PAUL & PETER ARE CHOSEN (Lesson #3)

❏ Read Acts 12:20-25

> *What struck you?*

> *What might God be saying to you?*

❏ Prayer

> *Pray for boldness in your witness.*
> *Pray for the leaders of your church.*
> *Pray for your list.*
> *Who?*   *What?*

❏ I will fast today.

❏ I am going to connect w/ (visit, phone, email, facebook, note, card, have over) _____ today.

❏ Questions:

1. The historian Josephus tells of the festival Herod celebrated honoring Claudius Caesar. He describes the silver robe Herod wore and how the people called him a god. He also tells how Herod got violent pains and died 5 days later. How do we sometimes try to be our own god? Why is this so offensive to God?

Sermon or Bible study notes on Lesson #3

Date: _____

Sermon or Bible study notes on Lesson #3

Date: _____

36

THE CHURCH EXPANDS (Lesson #4)

❑ Read Acts 13:1-52

What struck you?

What might God be saying to you?

❑ Prayer

Pray for boldness in your witness.
Pray for the leaders of your church.
Pray for your list.
Who?   *What?*

❑ I will fast today.

❑ I am going to connect w/ (visit, phone, email, facebook, note, card, have over) _____ today.

❑ Questions:

1. See Supplemental Material on Fasting, pg. 75.

2. How does the Holy Spirit direct us today?

3. What do you think God's purpose is for the time you have with your generation? (Verse 36)

4. Who in your world has a hard time accepting Jesus as the long awaited Messiah?

Date: _____

THE CHURCH EXPANDS (Lesson #4)

❑ Read Acts 14:1-20

> *What struck you?*

> *What might God be saying to you?*

❑ Prayer

> *Pray for boldness in your witness.*
> *Pray for the leaders of your church.*
> *Pray for your list.*
> *Who?*   *What?*

❑ I will fast today.

❑ I am going to connect w/ (visit, phone, email, facebook, note, card, have over) _____today.

❑ Question:

1. In the synagogue of a new city, Paul and Barnabas start sharing the gospel. They start with their own people - people who have the same problems and hangups as they once had. Can you identify who your own people would be - people who have the same problems and hangups you once had?

Date: _____

THE CHURCH EXPANDS (Lesson #4)

❑ Read Acts 14:21-28

> *What struck you?*

> *What might God be saying to you?*

❑ Prayer

> *Pray for boldness in your witness.*
> *Pray for the leaders of your church.*
> *Pray for your list.*
> *Who?*   *What?*

❑ I will fast today.

❑ I am going to connect w/ (visit, phone, email, facebook, note, card, have over) _____today.

❑ Questions:

1. Elders were appointed in each church. Why is this important?

2. How can you help the leaders of your church?

3. In what area of the church might God be calling you to be a leader?

Date: _____

THE CHURCH EXPANDS (Lesson #4)

❏ Read Acts 15:1-21

> *What struck you?*

> *What might God be saying to you?*

❏ Prayer

> *Pray for boldness in your witness.*
> *Pray for the leaders of your church.*
> *Pray for your list.*
> *Who?*   *What?*

❏ I will fast today.

❏ I am going to connect w/ (visit, phone, email, facebook, note, card, have over) _____ today.

❏ Questions:

1. Why is it sometimes difficult when new-to-the-faith Christians join in with old-to-the-faith Christians?

2. What do you think of the compromise that this church council came up with in verses 19-21?

3. How does one balance law and grace?

Date: _____

THE CHURCH EXPANDS (Lesson #4)

❑ Read Acts 15:22-41

What struck you?

What might God be saying to you?

❑ Prayer

Pray for boldness in your witness.
Pray for the leaders of your church.
Pray for your list.
Who?   *What?*

❑ I will fast today.

❑ I am going to connect w/ (visit, phone, email, facebook, note, card, have over) _____today.

❑ Questions:

1. What role does the Holy Spirit (vs. 28) play in settling disputes?

2. Why are there sometimes "sharp disputes" even among church people?

3. How can we disagree with each other and at the same time focus on God's mission, His purpose?

Date: _____

THE CHURCH EXPANDS (Lesson #4)

❑ Read Acts 16:1-15

> *What struck you?*

> *What might God be saying to you?*

❑ Prayer

> *Pray for boldness in your witness.*
> *Pray for the leaders of your church.*
> *Pray for your list.*
> *Who?*   *What?*

❑ I will fast today.

❑ I am going to connect w/ (visit, phone, email, facebook, note, card, have over) _____today.

❑ Questions:

1. You have been praying for boldness in your witness, for your church and its leaders, for your list of people you know who need a closer walk with the Lord, and for specific people about their specific struggles. How has the Holy Spirit directed you in these things?

2. Who needs their heart opened in your world? (Verse 14)

THE CHURCH EXPANDS (Lesson #4)

❑ Read Acts 16:16-40

> *What struck you?*

> *What might God be saying to you?*

❑ Prayer

> *Pray for boldness in your witness.*
> *Pray for the leaders of your church.*
> *Pray for your list.*
> *Who?*   *What?*

❑ I will fast today.

❑ I am going to connect w/ (visit, phone, email, facebook, note, card, have over) _____today.

❑ Questions:

1. What do you think Paul meant by the word, "Believe?" (Verse 31)

2. "... he and his whole family." In what way is Christianity a family affair? (Verse 34)

3. How is the faith being passed on in your family?

Date: _____

Sermon or Bible study notes on Lesson #4

Date: _____

Sermon or Bible study notes on Lesson #4

Date: _____

THE CHURCH EXPLODES (Lesson #5)
❑ Read Acts 17:1-34

> What struck you?

> What might God be saying to you?

❑ Prayer

> Pray for boldness in your witness.
>
> Pray for the leaders of your church.
>
> Pray for your list.
>
> Who?   What?
>
> Pray for an open door to someone's life.

❑ I will fast today.

❑ I am going to connect w/ (visit, phone, email, facebook, note, card, have over) _____today.

❑ Questions:

1. What do the Bereans and the people of your church share?

2. Paul "reasoned" in the synagogue and the market-place. How can you reach people in your church and in the marketplace?

3. How are the people you know, who don't go to church, religious? How can you reach them? (Verse 22)

Date: _____

THE CHURCH EXPLODES (Lesson #5)

❑ Read Acts 18:1-17

> *What struck you?*

> *What might God be saying to you?*

❑ Prayer

> *Pray for boldness in your witness.*
> *Pray for the leaders of your church.*
> *Pray for your list.*
> *Who?*   *What?*
> *Pray for an open door to someone's life.*
> *Pray for people God is already working on in your city.*

❑ I will fast today.

❑ I am going to connect w/ (visit, phone, email, facebook, note, card, have over) _____ today.

❑ Questions:

1. Even though Paul often says he is done sharing the gospel with the Jews because it never goes well, he keeps trying. Why do you think that is? (Verse 6)

2. See page 76 for supplemental Bible Study material Three for you and/or your small group. (Verse 9,10)

Date: _____

THE CHURCH EXPLODES (Lesson #5)

❑ Read Acts 18:18-28

> *What struck you?*

> *What might God be saying to you?*

❑ Prayer

> *Pray for boldness in your witness.*
> *Pray for the leaders of your church.*
> *Pray for your list.*
> *Who?   What?*
> *Pray for an open door to someone's life.*
> *Pray for people God is already working on in your city.*

❑ I will fast today.

❑ I am going to connect w/ (visit, phone, email, facebook, note, card, have over) _____today.

❑ Questions:

1. Paul and believers like Priscilla and Aquila spent a lot of their time convincing people, from the Scriptures, that Jesus was the Christ, the long-awaited Messiah. Why was this so important?

2. How would you explain to someone that Jesus is the Christ, the long-awaited Messiah?

THE CHURCH EXPLODES (Lesson #5)

❑ Read Acts 19:1-22

> *What struck you?*
>
>
>
>

> *What might God be saying to you?*
>
>
>
>

❑ Prayer

> *Pray for boldness in your witness.*
>
> *Pray for the leaders of your church.*
>
> *Pray for your list.*
>
> *Who?   What?*
>
> *Pray for an open door to someone's life.*
>
> *Pray for people God is already working on in your city.*

❑ I will fast today.

❑ I am going to connect w/ (visit, phone, email, facebook, note, card, have over) _____today.

❑ Questions:

1. What do you think it means to receive the Holy Spirit when one is baptized into the name of Jesus?

2. Christianity was known as the WAY. Why would that be? (Verse 9)

3. How is your church on the path to a Jesus **way**?

Date: _____

THE CHURCH EXPLODES (Lesson #5)

❑ Read Acts 19:23-41

> What struck you?

> What might God be saying to you?

❑ Prayer

> Pray for boldness in your witness.
>
> Pray for the leaders of your church.
>
> Pray for your list.
>
> Who?   What?
>
> Pray for an open door to someone's life.
>
> Pray for people God is already working on in your city.

❑ I will fast today.

❑ I am going to connect w/ (visit, phone, email, facebook, note, card, have over) _____today.

❑ Questions:

1. The temple of Artemis was one of the seven wonders of the world. Why were the people of Ephesus so afraid of Christianity?

2. You can go to the same outdoor theater (holds 5,000 people) today. Would we have the enthusiasm to cry out "Great is the Lord, God Almighty" for two hours?

THE CHURCH EXPLODES (Lesson #5)

❏ Read Acts 20:1-12

> *What struck you?*

> *What might God be saying to you?*

❏ Prayer

> *Pray for boldness in your witness.*
> *Pray for the leaders of your church.*
> *Pray for your list.*
> *Who?   What?*
> *Pray for an open door to someone's life.*
> *Pray for people God is already working on in your city.*

❏ I will fast today.

❏ I am going to connect w/ (visit, phone, email, facebook, note, card, have over) _____today.

❏ Questions:

1. Why would people stay up all night to listen to Paul?

2. Have you ever fallen asleep in church?

3. After Eutychus was raised from the dead, Paul kept talking until the next morning. Can we get this kind of enthusiasm for God, His Word, His people, and His mission?

Date: _____

THE CHURCH EXPLODES (Lesson #5)

❑ Read Acts 20:13-38

> *What struck you?*

> *What might God be saying to you?*

❑ Prayer

> *Pray for boldness in your witness.*
> *Pray for the leaders of your church.*
> *Pray for your list.*
> *Who?   What?*
> *Pray for an open door to someone's life.*
> *Pray for people God is already working on in your city.*

❑ I will fast today.

❑ I am going to connect w/ (visit, phone, email, facebook, note, card, have over) _____today.

❑ Questions:

1. What do you make of "house to house?" (Verse 20)

2. Try praying vs. 24 for your own prayer.

3. Paul warns of trouble, not only from outside of the church, but from inside as well. (Verses 30, 31) Have you seen this? What can we do about it?

Date: _____

Sermon or Bible study notes on Lesson #5

Date: _____

Sermon or Bible study notes on Lesson #5

Date: _____

THE CHURCH ON TRIAL (Lesson #6)

❑ Read Acts 21:1-40

> *What struck you?*

> *What might God be saying to you?*

❑ Prayer

> *Pray for boldness in your witness.*
> *Pray for the leaders of your church.*
> *Pray for your list.*
> *Who?*   *What?*
> *Pray for an open door to someone's life.*
> *Pray for people God is already working on in your city.*

❑ I will fast today.

❑ I am going to connect w/ (visit, phone, email, facebook, note, card, have over) _____today.

❑ Questions:

1. The disciples and their wives and children knelt on the beach to pray. Why does this sound good? (Verse 5)

2. Where could you kneel down to pray in a public place that might be a stretch for you?

3. Why do think Paul was so adamant about going to Jerusalem?

Date: _____

THE CHURCH ON TRIAL (Lesson #6)

❑ Read Acts 22:1-21

> *What struck you?*

> *What might God be saying to you?*

❑ Prayer

> *Pray for boldness in your witness.*
>
> *Pray for the leaders of your church.*
>
> *Pray for your list.*
>
> *Who?   What?*
>
> *Pray for an open door to someone's life.*
>
> *Pray for people God is already working on in your city.*

❑ I will fast today.

❑ I am going to connect w/ (visit, phone, email, facebook, note, card, have over) _____ today.

❑ Questions:

1. Paul gives this same testimony every chance he gets. It is a testimony of what Jesus did and how he did it for Paul. What is your testimony?

2. Paul explains why he went to the Gentiles. Who have you been sent to?

Date: _____

THE CHURCH ON TRIAL (Lesson #6)

❑ Read Acts 22:22-29

> *What struck you?*

> *What might God be saying to you?*

❑ Prayer

> *Pray for boldness in your witness.*
> *Pray for the leaders of your church.*
> *Pray for your list.*
> *Who?   What?*
> *Pray for an open door to someone's life.*
> *Pray for people God is already working on in your city.*

❑ I will fast today.

❑ I am going to connect w/ (visit, phone, email, facebook, note, card, have over) _____today.

❑ Questions:

1. The people wanted Paul dead. What is the worst persecution that you have received for your faith? (Verse 22)

2. Persecution can come from inside the church or the government. How are either or both persecuting the church today?

57

Date: _____

THE CHURCH ON TRIAL (Lesson #6)

❑ Read Acts 22:30 - Acts 23:11

> *What struck you?*

> *What might God be saying to you?*

❑ Prayer

> *Pray for boldness in your witness.*
> *Pray for the leaders of your church.*
> *Pray for your list.*
> *Who?   What?*
> *Pray for an open door to someone's life.*
> *Pray for people God is already working on in your city.*

❑ I will fast today.

❑ I am going to connect w/ (visit, phone, email, facebook, note, card, have over) _____ today.

❑ Questions:

1. It doesn't start out well before the Sanhedrin. Paul apologizes. What do think about that?

2. What is the point of religion if there is no resurrection?

3. Has God ever spoken to you? (Verse 11)

Date: _____

THE CHURCH ON TRIAL (Lesson #6)

❑ Read Acts 23:12-35

> *What struck you?*

> *What might God be saying to you?*

❑ Prayer

> *Pray for boldness in your witness.*
>
> *Pray for the leaders of your church.*
>
> *Pray for your list.*
>
> *Who?*   *What?*
>
> *Pray for an open door to someone's life.*
>
> *Pray for people God is already working on in your city.*

❑ I will fast today.

❑ I am going to connect w/ (visit, phone, email, facebook, note, card, have over) _____ today.

❑ Questions:

1. It seems that Paul was being protected by the secular government from the death threats of the religious rulers. What is going on here?

2. How do you think Paul felt through all of this?

Date: _____

THE CHURCH ON TRIAL (Lesson #6)

❑ Read Acts 24:1-9

> *What struck you?*

> *What might God be saying to you?*

❑ Prayer

> *Pray for boldness in your witness.*
>
> *Pray for the leaders of your church.*
>
> *Pray for your list.*
>
> *Who?   What?*
>
> *Pray for an open door to someone's life.*
>
> *Pray for people God is already working on in your city.*

❑ I will fast today.

❑ I am going to connect w/ (visit, phone, email, facebook, note, card, have over) _____today.

❑ Questions:

1. Tertullus seems to be sucking up to the government leaders. Is this good or not?

2. Paul is called a "ringleader" of the Nazarene sect. In what way is Christianity a sect and in what way are you a ringleader in it?

THE CHURCH ON TRIAL (Lesson #6)

❏ Read Acts 24:10-27

> What struck you?

> What might God be saying to you?

❏ Prayer

> Pray for boldness in your witness.
>
> Pray for the leaders of your church.
>
> Pray for your list.
>
> Who?   What?
>
> Pray for an open door to someone's life.
>
> Pray for people God is already working on in your city.

❏ I will fast today.

❏ I am going to connect w/ (visit, phone, email, facebook, note, card, have over) _____today.

❏ Questions:

1. What do you think of Paul's defense?
2. Why do you think Felix kept Paul in prison for two years?
3. When have you felt like you were in prison?

Date: _____

Sermon or Bible study notes on Lesson #6

Date: _____

Sermon or Bible study notes on Lesson #6

Date: _____

THE CHURCH ON THE WORLD STAGE (Lesson #7)

❑ Read Acts 25:1-27

> *What struck you?*

> *What might God be saying to you?*

❑ Prayer

> *Pray for boldness in your witness.*
> *Pray for the leaders of your church.*
> *Pray for your list.*
> *Who?   What?*
> *Pray for an open door to someone's life.*
> *Pray for people God is already working on in your city.*

❑ I will fast today.

❑ I am going to connect w/ (visit, phone, email, facebook, note, card, have over) _____ today.

❑ Questions:

1. Paul's life seemed to be in the hands of those who were more interested in politics than in truth. Have you ever been in that situation?

2. What is sad about this situation where Paul has to appeal to Ceasar to be saved?

THE CHURCH ON THE WORLD STAGE (Lesson #7)

❑ Read Acts 26:1-18

> *What struck you?*

> *What might God be saying to you?*

❑ Prayer

> *Pray for boldness in your witness.*
> *Pray for the leaders of your church.*
> *Pray for your list.*
> *Who?   What?*
> *Pray for an open door to someone's life.*
> *Pray for people God is already working on in your city.*

❑ I will fast today.

❑ I am going to connect w/ (visit, phone, email, facebook, note, card, have over) _____today.

❑ Questions:

1. Paul gives his testimony yet again. What would be your unique testimony?

2. What do you think Paul meant by "... rescue you from your own people and the Gentiles?" (Verse 17)

Date: _____

THE CHURCH ON THE WORLD STAGE (Lesson #7)

❑ Read Acts 26:19-32

> *What struck you?*

> *What might God be saying to you?*

❑ Prayer

> *Pray for boldness in your witness.*
> *Pray for the leaders of your church.*
> *Pray for your list.*
> *Who?   What?*
> *Pray for an open door to someone's life.*
> *Pray for people God is already working on in your city.*

❑ I will fast today.

❑ I am going to connect w/ (visit, phone, email, facebook, note, card, have over) _____today.

❑ Questions:

1. Paul had a clear vision from God. What is your clear vision from God? (Verse 19)

2. Why do think Festus thought Paul was out of his mind? (Verse 24)

3. Why do think King Agrippa asked this? (Verse 28)

THE CHURCH ON THE WORLD STAGE (Lesson #7)

❑ Read Acts 27:1-26

> *What struck you?*

> *What might God be saying to you?*

❑ Prayer

> *Pray for boldness in your witness.*
>
> *Pray for the leaders of your church.*
>
> *Pray for your list.*
>
> *Who?   What?*
>
> *Pray for an open door to someone's life.*
>
> *Pray for people God is already working on in your city.*

❑ I will fast today.

❑ I am going to connect w/ (visit, phone, email, facebook, note, card, have over) _____today.

❑ Questions:

1. How well do you receive the advice of others? (Verse 21)

2. What do you think the secular men on the ship thought of Paul's little speech?

3. When have you made such a speech of God's good-ness and faithfulness in a difficult situation in front of

Date: _____

THE CHURCH ON THE WORLD STAGE (Lesson #7)

❑ Read Acts 27:27-44

> *What struck you?*

> *What might God be saying to you?*

❑ Prayer

> *Pray for boldness in your witness.*
>
> *Pray for the leaders of your church.*
>
> *Pray for your list.*
>
> *Who?   What?*
>
> *Pray for an open door to someone's life.*
>
> *Pray for people God is already working on in your city.*

❑ I will fast today.

❑ I am going to connect w/ (visit, phone, email, facebook, note, card, have over) _____today.

❑ Questions:

1. Why do think the centurion listened and gave in to Paul's advice? (Verses 30-32)

2. Paul seems to have become the leader of a large group of people. How do you think he did it? (Verse 37)

3. Should we strive for leadership?

THE CHURCH ON THE WORLD STAGE (Lesson #7)

❑ Read Acts 28:1-10

> *What struck you?*

> *What might God be saying to you?*

❑ Prayer

> *Pray for boldness in your witness.*
> *Pray for the leaders of your church.*
> *Pray for your list.*
> *Who?   What?*
> *Pray for an open door to someone's life.*
> *Pray for people God is already working on in your city.*

❑ I will fast today.

❑ I am going to connect w/ (visit, phone, email, facebook, note, card, have over) _____today.

❑ Questions:

1. It is interesting that Paul does many miracles on the Island of Malta but we hear of no miracles on board the ship. Why might this be?

2. Verse 7 speaks of hospitality. Why not invite someone over for dinner? Who could you invite?

Date: _____

THE CHURCH ON THE WORLD STAGE (Lesson #7)

❑ Read Acts 28:11- 31

> *What struck you?*

> *What might God be saying to you?*

❑ Prayer

> *Pray for boldness in your witness.*
>
> *Pray for the leaders of your church.*
>
> *Pray for your list.*
>
> *Who?   What?*
>
> *Pray for an open door to someone's life.*
>
> *Pray for people God is already working on in your city.*

❑ I will fast today.

❑ I am going to connect w/ (visit, phone, email, facebook, note, card, have over) _____today.

❑ Questions:

1. Paul was met by some of the "brothers" who escorted him to Rome. Why would that be a comfort to Paul?

2. When have you had to face a difficult and uncertain situation and were encouraged by brothers and sisters who rallied around to support you?

Sermon or Bible study notes on Lesson #7

Date: _____

Sermon or Bible study notes on Lesson #7

1. Who has been like Philip to you, teaching you the Word of God? _____.

2. How have you been like the Ethiopian? A. Eager to learn. B. Confused. C. Ready to make commitments. D. Other _____.

3. Just as God put the Ethiopian on the same path as Philip, God has put people on your path as well. Here is a list of connections the average person has. Read the list. Then write down any names that come to mind of people in your life that are like the Ethiopian - needing a walk with God and a stronger connection to church

> Spouse, children, parents, siblings, cousins, banker, teacher, co-worker, neighbor, old friend, sports or hobby friends, school connections, kids connections, sales or cash register people, waiter, craft friends, classmates, teammates, business connections, mailman, hair-cutter, people at the gym, facebook connections, anyone who knows your name and you know their name.

_____ _____ _____

_____ _____ _____

_____ _____ _____

_____ _____ _____

_____ _____

Out of your big list, choose three or four individuals that you will pray for every day for the rest of this series.

_____ _____ _____

_____ _____ _____

Acts 13:2,3 While they were worshiping the Lord and fasting, the Holy Spirit said, "Set apart for me Barnabas and Saul for the work to which I have called them." So after they had fasted and prayed, they placed their hands on them and sent them off.

Fasting is withdrawing from food for a set period of time (part of a day, a day, maybe two, sometimes longer).

❑ **How might the resulting hunger (from the fast) help you ...**

1. Get more in tune with God' Spirit?

2. Worship God?

3. Make group decisions as in Acts 13:2,3?

❑ **Have you ever fasted for religious purposes? If not, why not? If so, how did it go?**

Fasting is a great way to wait on the Lord for direction - in your church, in your marriage, in your family, or in your business. It is a great way to start a new season of life or a new year. Fasting helps a person focus on real needs and what really matters.

❑ **Can you...**

1. Give fasting at least one try?
2. Come up with a fasting plan (i.e. one meal a week, one day a week, etc.)?

❑ **Record any insights or interesting obervations about your fasting experience somewhere in this booklet and then share at your next small group meeting.**

Supplemental Material Three: Acts 18:9-10

Acts 18:9-10 One night the Lord spoke to Paul in a vision: "Do not be afraid; keep on speaking, do not be silent. 10 For I am with you, and no one is going to attack and harm you, because I have many people in this city."

❑ **"Do not be afraid ..."**

What are you afraid of when it comes to inviting someone to church?

1. "I am not comfortable with new people period."

2. "I am afraid of rejection."

3. "I am afraid they might come to church and I will be worried about them the whole time."

4. "I am afraid I don't know anyone well enough to invite them to church."

❑ **"... keep on speaking, do not be silent."**

How do you feel about sharing your faith?

1. "I don't know how - or even if I did know how - I don't feel comfortable talking about God and Church."

2. "I would love to share my faith if the other person brings it up."

3. "I do it all the time."

❑ **"For I am with you ..."**

How does knowing God is with you help in inviting someone to church and talking to someone about your faith?

❑ **"I have many people in this city"**

How does knowing that God is already at work in the lives of people you want to invite to church and/or share your faith with give you resolve and confidence to invite and share?

Congratulations on finishing the Acts Bible Study.

If you want some ideas on what to do next, check out other CLI Bible studies at

www.christianleadersinstitute.org/shop

CLI Ministry Bible Studies

CLI Bible Study Tools/Sermon Series

Genesis: The Foundation of Everything (Books 1,2,3,4)

Acts: The Unbelievable Story of the Church

Ephesians: Who are you

Daniel: Hope When Things Seem Hopeless

The 7 Things Every Christian Should Know

Lead Like Jesus

Christmas Advent Bible Study

7 Favorite Bible Stories that Kids Love

Lifestyles of the Jesus Way

CLI Bible Study/Retreat Series

Marriage Connection:
Tips from a Guy Married 700 Times
The Man-Up Bible Study

CLI Bible Study/Book Series

Being a Lifeboat Church in a Cruiseship Titanic World
Philemon: How to Win Friends &Tactfully
Get Along with People
The Secret of a Great Music Ministry Questions
The Secret to a Great Preaching Ministry Questions
The Secret to a Great Evangelism Ministry Questions
The Jesus Bible
The 30 Second Bible
Building a Walk-with-God Church

CLI Walk-with-God Bible Studies

How to Get a Personal Walk with God
How to Get a Marriage Walk with God
How to Get a Family Walk with God
How to Help Others Get a Walk with God
How to Use Hospitality to Share Your Walk with God

**Check out these and other ministry resources at
www.christianleadersinstitute.org/Biblestudytools**

Made in the USA
Columbia, SC
23 April 2018